THE SUPREME COURT

THE U.S. GOVERNMENT
HOW IT WORKS

★ ★ ★

THE CENTRAL INTELLIGENCE AGENCY
THE DEPARTMENT OF HOMELAND SECURITY
THE FEDERAL BUREAU OF INVESTIGATION
THE HOUSE OF REPRESENTATIVES
THE PRESIDENCY
THE SENATE
THE SUPREME COURT

THE U.S. GOVERNMENT
HOW IT WORKS

THE SUPREME COURT

HEATHER LEHR WAGNER

CHELSEA HOUSE
PUBLISHERS
An imprint of Infobase Publishing

The Supreme Court

Chelsea House
An imprint of Infobase Publishing
132 West 31st Street
New York, NY 10001

ISBN-10: 0-7910-9283-6
ISBN-13: 978-0-7910-9283-5

Library of Congress Cataloging-in-Publication Data

Wagner, Heather Lehr.
   The Supreme Court / Heather Lehr Wagner.
      p. cm. — (The U.S. government : how it works)
   Includes bibliographical references and index.
   ISBN 0-7910-9283-6 (hardcover)
   1. United States. Supreme Court—Juvenile literature. [1. United States. Supreme Court.] I. Title. II. Series.

   KF8742.Z9W34 2007
   347.73'26—dc22

                            2006028510

CONTENTS

1

A Visit to the Supreme Court

On the morning of December 8, 1953, the Court Chamber of the Supreme Court of the United States was crowded with spectators. Many had waited in line since before dawn to witness the Supreme Court hear the final arguments in the case of *Brown v. Board of Education of Topeka*.

Brown v. Board of Education was actually five separate lawsuits, all filed by African-American students and their parents to challenge the segregation of students in local public schools. The cases involved the actions of school boards not only in Topeka, Kansas, but also in Delaware, the District of Columbia, South Carolina, and Virginia.

The cases involved different states but had one central issue in common: Is it constitutional to provide

African-American children arrived for class in 1953 at the segregated Buchanan Elementary School in Topeka, Kansas—one of the schools cited in *Brown v. Board of Education of Topeka*. The *Brown* case was actually five separate lawsuits challenging the constitutionality of the segregation of schools. The U.S. Supreme Court unanimously ruled that segregation deprived students of equal education.

separate schools for children of different races (segregated schools)? In one of the cases—the original *Brown v. Board of Education of Topeka*—parents tried to enroll their children in schools in their neighborhood and were refused because their children were not white. Instead, they were told that their children would need to attend one of the four schools in the city for African Americans. Many of these schools were located far from the children's homes, requiring them to travel a long distance by bus.

Another of the cases began with a strike organized by a high school student named Barbara Rose Johns. Johns and her fellow students had protested the conditions at their school—it had no gym, no cafeteria, and no restroom for teachers. The school, which was in Prince Edward County, Virginia, was so crowded that some students were being taught in an old school bus and three old buildings covered with tar paper. A lawsuit was filed on behalf of 117 students when protests to the local school board failed to produce any effort to improve the conditions in the school.

Because the cases all involved segregation, they had been grouped together when they reached the Supreme Court. The cases became jointly known as *Brown v. Board of Education of Topeka*.

On that December morning, attorney Thurgood Marshall was seated at one of the long tables reserved for lawyers arguing cases before the Supreme Court. The 45-year-old Marshall was representing those who had originally filed the suits against their school boards, as an attorney for the National Association for the Advancement of Colored People (NAACP). The NAACP had focused on fighting racial discrimination for several years. Recently, the NAACP had begun to concentrate on issues involving educational equality, working to ensure that African Americans received improved schooling.

Marshall had appeared before the Supreme Court a year earlier for the initial hearing of the *Brown v. Board of Education* case. Marshall had gathered evidence from a large group of experts. This evidence demonstrated that black and white children had equal learning potential but that black children's self-esteem and motivation to learn dropped dramatically when they were segregated in what were generally inferior schools. Marshall's argument was that school segregation had no legal basis.

The nine justices of the Supreme Court had requested a rehearing of the case in order to give them additional time to consider an issue that would have impact on schools across the country. The rehearing began on December 7. One day later, Marshall was prepared to offer his final arguments in the case.

It was Marshall's fifteenth appearance before the Supreme Court, but it was clear that this was the most important case of his career. As the day's session began, Marshall, along with everyone in the Chamber, rose to his feet and stared straight ahead as the red velvet curtains at the front of the courtroom opened. Nine black-robed men stepped through the curtain and took their place at the long bench, and the final arguments in the case of *Brown v. Board of Education* were delivered. In his final argument, Marshall noted, "The only thing [segregation] can be is an inherent determination that the people who were formerly in slavery, regardless of anything else, shall be kept as near that stage as possible. And now is the time, we submit, that this court should make it clear that this is not what our Constitution stands for."

The Supreme Court did not deliver its final decision on that day. As with every case, the justices discussed the case in private, and it was not until five months later—on May 17, 1954—that the Supreme Court delivered its opinion, ruling unanimously that segregation deprived minority children of equal educational opportunities. In one ruling, the Supreme Court had transformed the system of education in the United States.

AT FIRST GLANCE

In the earliest days of America's history as an independent country, those charged with shaping the new nation divided the government into three branches—the executive branch, whose power was concentrated in the office of president of the United States; the legislative branch, where power was centralized in the U.S. Congress; and the judicial branch, whose highest court was known as the Supreme Court of the United States. In describing the limits and scope of these three branches, the Constitution was quite specific regarding the powers of the president and Congress. It was the description of the limits and powers of the judicial branch that was vague and brief. The details of exactly what role the Supreme Court would assume in the American political system would be filled in by history.

A visitor to the U.S. Supreme Court today can sense its power and majesty. The white marble building faces the U.S. Capitol on its west side, where the main entrance is located. Walking toward the first set of low steps, one sees on either side a pair of marble candelabra on square bases. On these bases, carvings show a representation of *Justice*, holding a sword and scales, and *The Three Fates*, shown weaving the legendary thread of life. These low steps lead up to a 252-foot-wide oval plaza, with fountains, flagpoles, and benches placed on either side.

IN THE CONSTITUTION

★ ★ ★ ★ ★

The judicial branch of the United States is addressed in Article III of the U.S. Constitution. The following is Section 1 of Article III:

The judicial power of the United States, shall be vested in one Supreme Court, and in such inferior courts as the Congress may from time to time ordain and establish. The judges, both of the supreme and inferior courts, shall hold their offices during good behaviour, and shall, at stated times, receive for their services, a compensation, which shall not be diminished during their continuance in office.

A second set of steps leads up to the main entrance. Guarding the two sides of the steps are two large figures sculpted from marble by James Earle Fraser. A woman is on the left, described as *The Contemplation of Justice.* On the right is a man, known as *The Guardian* or *Authority of Law.*

Sixteen marble columns line the main entrance. Above them is carved a phrase meant to symbolize the mission of the U.S. Supreme Court: "Equal Justice Under Law."

After climbing the steps, a visitor walks through a set of opened bronze doors. These doors each weigh six and a half tons. When the entrance is open, the doors slide into a recess in the wall. Panels on the doors show scenes from the history of the creation of laws, including scenes from Greek, Roman, and British history, as well as images of Chief Justice John Marshall and Justice Joseph Story, two influential figures from the early days of the U.S. Supreme Court.

After moving through the entranceway, a visitor enters the Great Hall, where two rows of marble columns rise to the ceiling. All of the former chief justices of the Supreme Court are represented in busts set along the side wall.

At the east end of the Great Hall, oak doors mark the entrance to the Court Chamber, where the Supreme Court meets when in session. This impressive room has a 44-foot-high (13.4-meter-high) ceiling, and the room itself measures 82 by 91 feet (25 by 28 meters). A total of 24 marble columns line this room, and the walls and floor borders are also made of marble. Above the columns on

Marble columns grace the main entrance to the U.S. Supreme Court building in Washington, D.C. Above the columns, the phrase "Equal Justice Under Law" adorns the entrance. Those words reflect the mission of the court.

the east and west walls, two marble panels depict several historical lawgivers.

The nine justices of the Supreme Court (one chief justice and eight associate justices) sit behind a raised mahogany bench during public sessions. The bench was originally straight, but it was changed in 1972 to a half-hexagon shape, described as "winged," to offer better sound and visibility for the justices. A large clock hangs on a chain behind the bench, between two marble columns.

To the left of the bench is a desk for the clerk of the court. The clerk is in charge of administering the schedule of cases that the Supreme Court will hear and also oversees the admission of lawyers to the Supreme Court Bar. To the right of the bench is a desk for the marshal of the court, who serves as timekeeper of court sessions. The marshal signals lawyers presenting cases before the court with white and red lights, which tell them of time limits for their presentations and when time has expired. The marshal also manages the court building, supervising security and maintenance.

In front of the bench are a series of mahogany tables. These are for the lawyers who are arguing cases before the court. When it is their turn to present their arguments, these attorneys make their presentations to the court from a lectern in the center.

A bronze railing divides the room, neatly separating the attorneys and justices from the public. In the public section, red benches on the left side of the courtroom are for the media. On the right are red benches for guests of the justices. Black chairs in front of those benches are for officers of the court and visiting dignitaries.

Many of the practices conducted when the Supreme Court is in session have been shaped by history. Tradition plays an important role in the court's activities. One of these unexpected traditions is the placing of white goose-quill pens on the lawyers' tables each day that the court is in session.

When a court session begins, the nine black-robed justices step through red velvet drapes and take their places at the bench. They are seated according to seniority in high-back, black-leather chairs. The chief justice sits in the center chair; the senior (longest-serving) associate justice sits to his right, the second senior to his left, and so on, alternating left and right based on the number of years a justice has served on the court.

A gavel sounds loudly through the courtroom and all those present stand and remain standing while the marshal loudly calls out, "Oyez! Oyez! Oyez! All persons having business before the Honorable, the Supreme Court of the United States, are admonished to draw near and give their attention, for the Court is now sitting. God save the United States and this Honorable Court."

With this cry, another session of the U.S. Supreme Court begins.

A HISTORY THAT SHAPED AMERICA

A review of the cases that have been presented before the U.S. Supreme Court offers a nearly comprehensive account of the issues that have shaped American history. In *Marbury v. Madison* (1803), the Supreme Court asserted its right to overturn unconstitutional legislation if needed to uphold the Constitution. This case firmly established the Supreme Court's role as an independent branch of government charged with upholding and interpreting the Constitution, even if it meant that the Supreme Court must oppose the actions of Congress or the president.

McCulloch v. Maryland (1819) affirmed the right of Congress to charter a national bank and limited the power of individual states to tax the proceeds of such a bank. The

Dred Scott case (1857) declared that African Americans were not eligible to become citizens and that Congress could not halt the spread of slavery. In *American Communications Association v. Douds* (1950), the court upheld a requirement that all labor union officers swear that they were not members of the Communist Party.

The 1954 landmark decision of *Brown v. Board of Education of Topeka* stated that public schools could not be segregated by race, that the concept of "separate but equal" had no place in public education. In 1966, the court ruled in *Miranda v. Arizona* that the police may not interrogate a suspect in custody unless they have informed him of his right to remain silent, of the fact that his words may be used against him, and of his right to a lawyer. And in 1974, in *United States v. Nixon*, the court determined that President Richard Nixon must comply with a request for taped recordings of conversations in the White House in an investigation of former White House aides. As a result of information disclosed in these tapes, Nixon was forced to resign his office that same year to avoid impeachment.

Many of the issues that continue to spark national debate were decided in the Supreme Court. The issues of prayer in schools, the death penalty, government use of electronic surveillance without a warrant, abortion, and discrimination have all been shaped because of rulings by the Supreme Court.

The nine individuals who serve as justices of the Supreme Court are appointed by the president, and the length of their terms is restricted in the Constitution only

Ernesto Miranda was the plaintiff in the landmark case
Miranda v. Arizona. In 1966, the Supreme Court ruled that
the police may not interrogate a suspect in custody unless
they have informed him of his right to remain silent, of his
right to a lawyer, and other rights. These rights have become
known as Miranda rights.

by the phrase, "[they] shall hold their offices during good behaviour." The men and women who have served as justices of the Supreme Court have been appointed by presidents who hoped to achieve a certain "balance" in the court or to ensure a court that adhered to a particular political philosophy. Justices, however, generally remain on the court long after the presidents who appointed them have left office. The court's rulings are a result of lengthy discussions among the justices, and the opinions of both the majority and the minority are made public once a decision has been handed down.

The words that appear above the main entrance to the Supreme Court—"Equal Justice Under Law"—reflect the court's responsibility to serve as the highest court in America. By protecting the spirit of the Constitution and interpreting it when necessary, the court offers all Americans the opportunity for justice.

More than 7,000 civil and criminal cases are filed in the Supreme Court each year, from many federal and state courts. The justices decide which of these cases to hear, knowing that the cases they select—and the ultimate decisions reached by the court—will deeply impact the American legal system.

The Supreme Court is more than 200 years old, and yet only 17 men have served as chief justices, and fewer than 100 people have served as associate justices. To understand how these men and women make the decisions that shape America, it is helpful to first look back at the court's history and the cases that demonstrated its influence.

2

THE HISTORY
OF THE SUPREME
COURT

The foundations of the U.S. Supreme Court were first shaped by a group of men who gathered in Philadelphia in 1787. During several sweltering months in the city's State House, these men debated how a new federal government could be formed to ensure that the 13 new states could establish a union—a union that would cooperate economically and politically.

The 13 states had only recently been colonies—colonies that had won their independence from Great Britain in 1783. The first unifying system that had been created for these 13 states—the Articles of Confederation—had not proved successful. The states jealously guarded their independence and their right to make their own laws, resulting in a confusing system in which states fought over borders and trade. The states wanted their own money, their own laws, and their own rules to govern how and when business could be conducted. It was a mess, a mess that resulted in 13 weak, divided, quarreling states.

The men who met in Philadelphia in 1787 wanted something better for these newly independent states. They understood that a union needed to be created, a union that could restore some order to the chaos and ensure that those states continued to remain independent.

But as delegates from their respective states, those who attended the Constitutional Convention disagreed on how best to achieve a more perfect union. Some believed that a powerful, central government was needed, while others fought to preserve their state's power and right to govern itself. Some feared the creation of a powerful executive branch, believing it would inevitably lead to a monarchy. Others argued for a powerful Congress, where representatives from the individual states would make laws and shape policy. Slavery was yet another issue that divided the delegates.

Ultimately, the delegates created a system of government whose powers were divided into three separate areas: the executive (or president); the legislative (the U.S. Senate and the House of Representatives); and the judiciary (the U.S. Supreme Court). By and large, many more of their debates focused on the scope and shape of the executive and legislative branches. But the judiciary branch that was created from their debates would become extraordinarily powerful.

EARLY DEBATES

James Madison, a delegate from Virginia whose influence would be clearly felt in the Constitution that resulted from the convention, drafted what became known as the "Virginia Plan." Within the Virginia Plan was Madison's proposal for what he called a "national judiciary" whose powers would involve resolving "questions which may involve the national peace and harmony." He called for the creation of one or more "supreme tribunals" and several "inferior tribunals."

This vague proposal for the judiciary needed to be filled in, at least slightly, by the delegates. Madison had initially suggested that the legislative branch should choose the judges for these "tribunals," and several delegates supported him in this proposal. Other delegates, however, argued that these appointments should be made by the president (or the "national executive"). For instance, James Wilson of Pennsylvania argued that legislators might use an appointment to the "national judiciary" to reward their most faithful supporters. Coincidentally, Wilson would be rewarded in 1789 with a seat on the Supreme Court by George Washington.

One supporter of a legislative-appointed Supreme Court was John Rutledge of South Carolina, who was uncomfortable with the idea of an executive branch with too much

The influence of James Madison on the U.S. Constitution was strongly felt, although much of the focus of the Constitutional Convention of 1787 was on the executive and legislative branches of the government. The delegates spent little time discussing the judiciary. Even so, the judicial branch became a powerful one.

power, fearing that it would lead to monarchy. Giving the executive branch the power of judicial appointments would, Rutledge feared, add to an already powerful executive branch. It is interesting to note that Rutledge, too, would be appointed to the Supreme Court by George Washington.

As the debates continued, Madison suggested that perhaps judicial appointments should be made by the Senate, rather than by the entire Congress or by an individual executive. The issue was tabled for several weeks, as the Constitutional Convention focused on the legislative and executive branches.

Trying for a compromise, Madison suggested at one point that federal judges be appointed by the executive branch but that the support of at least one-third of the Senate would be required. The delegates did not initially back this proposal.

By August 1787, a draft of the Constitution had been prepared. This contained almost word for word what would become Article III of the Constitution—the article that establishes and details the jurisdiction of the Supreme Court. In the draft, the power to choose members of the Supreme Court was granted to the Senate. In the end, though, the Constitution gave the president the power to appoint the justices, with "the advice and consent" of the Senate.

The draft Constitution sparked continued discussion and debate, as delegates examined and revised the wording of every article. By August 27, it was time to examine Article III, and there was surprisingly little discussion or debate. It was agreed that the judicial power of the United States should be vested in a Supreme Court and to any "inferior courts" that might be created by the Congress. The Supreme Court was granted jurisdiction over "all cases under laws passed by the legislature of the United States," as well as any legal disputes between states, between a state and a citizen of another state, and between citizens of different states.

An amendment to the article was proposed during the August 27 debates by William Johnson of Connecticut. Johnson suggested that the Supreme Court should be given jurisdiction over "all cases arising under this Constitution" as well as laws enacted by Congress. This motion was quickly passed.

The result of this language was a Supreme Court with sweeping powers, perhaps far greater than the delegates realized as they focused with great zeal on limiting the powers of the executive branch. The Supreme Court, in the language approved in Article III of the Constitution, was given the power to strike down laws passed by Congress and the states if they were found to be in violation of the Constitution.

That power was further cemented in Article VI, known as the Supremacy Clause. In this article, the Constitution and federal laws are declared to be "the supreme law of the land; and the judges in every state shall be bound" by them. As the Supreme Court held the power to decide all cases arising under the Constitution, its decisions would become binding on every court throughout the country.

This power would inspire countless debates in the years that followed. This is the question of "judicial review"—whether the Supreme Court should have the right to review federal and state laws and strike down those laws that it determines are contrary to the Constitution. The Supreme Court has exercised this power, and hundreds of laws have been struck down because of it. For example, the Supreme Court has used this right to strike down laws that created segregated schools and state laws banning abortion. The Constitution that created the Supreme Court has also proved to be its most powerful judicial tool in shaping the laws of the United States.

THE FIRST COURT

On February 1, 1790, the Supreme Court of the United States had its first session. The question of how the justices would be dressed had caused some controversy. Judges in the English court system wore robes and white wigs. Some felt that the Supreme Court should continue that tradition, and one of the first justices, William Cushing, appeared at the first session wearing his old-fashioned wig. He was mercilessly teased in the streets of New York City as he walked to the Supreme Court and never wore the wig again, nor did any of the other justices.

The first session of the Supreme Court was held in the Royal Exchange Building in New York City, which was the nation's first capital. Many New York City lawyers turned up to see this historic first meeting of the Supreme Court. Unfortunately, only three of the six justices appeared on that day—the chief justice and two of the five associate justices. The number of justices had been set at six by Congress in the Judiciary Act of 1789, and at least four justices needed to be present for business to be legally conducted. With only three justices present, nothing could be done, and the court's first session was quickly adjourned.

The court's second day of business was hardly more impressive. This time a fourth justice appeared, and the court crier opened the session with the cry that would become the traditional opening for every Supreme Court session: "Oyez! Oyez! Oyez! All persons having business before the Honorable, the Supreme Court of the United States, are admonished to draw near and give their attention, for the Court is now sitting. God save the United States and this Honorable Court."

What followed this impressive declaration, however, was silence. No one had business before the court. The Supreme Court had no cases pending. To occupy their time, the four justices decided rules of procedure and rules for admitting lawyers to the court's bar.

Service on the Supreme Court was not considered the honor that it is today. The court had very few cases to decide in those early years. The pay was low. The court had crowded and unimpressive quarters in New York and in the second capital, Philadelphia. When the new capital was built in Washington, no building was set aside for the Supreme Court.

On top of the lack of prestige was the added burden of travel at a time when travel was difficult and time-consuming. The Judiciary Act of 1789 also required the

CHIEF JUSTICES OF THE SUPREME COURT

Chief Justice	Appointed by President	Years of Service
John Jay	George Washington	1789–1795
John Rutledge	George Washington	August–December 1795
Oliver Ellsworth	George Washington	1796–1800
John Marshall	John Adams	1801–1835
Roger Brooke Taney	Andrew Jackson	1836–1864
Salmon P. Chase	Abraham Lincoln	1864–1873
Morrison R. Waite	Ulysses S. Grant	1874–1888
Melville W. Fuller	Grover Cleveland	1888–1910
Edward D. White	William H. Taft	1910–1921

justices to sit on circuit courts that had been set up around the country. The states were divided into three circuits. The Middle Circuit consisted of New Jersey, Pennsylvania, Delaware, Maryland, and Virginia. The Southern Circuit encompassed North and South Carolina and Georgia. The Eastern Circuit contained New York and the New England states. Two Supreme Court justices were expected to hear cases at each of the circuit courts, requiring them to attend two sessions of the Supreme Court and then two

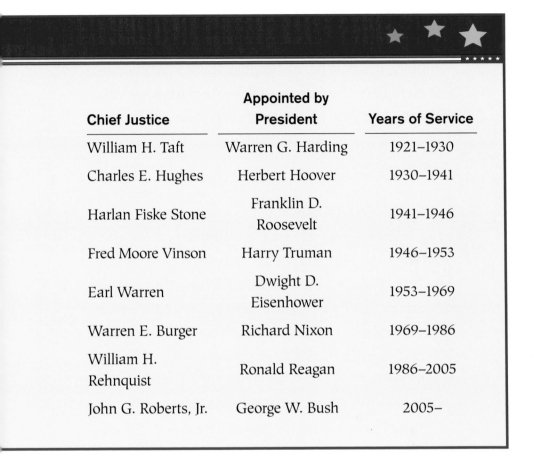

Chief Justice	Appointed by President	Years of Service
William H. Taft	Warren G. Harding	1921–1930
Charles E. Hughes	Herbert Hoover	1930–1941
Harlan Fiske Stone	Franklin D. Roosevelt	1941–1946
Fred Moore Vinson	Harry Truman	1946–1953
Earl Warren	Dwight D. Eisenhower	1953–1969
Warren E. Burger	Richard Nixon	1969–1986
William H. Rehnquist	Ronald Reagan	1986–2005
John G. Roberts, Jr.	George W. Bush	2005–

sessions of the circuit courts each year. Many of the early justices, including the first chief justice, John Jay, resigned their positions, claiming that the travel took them away from home for too long a period each year.

Another difficulty was that the justices could make a ruling in a circuit court, and then, if that ruling was appealed to the Supreme Court, they would be required to decide on the correctness of their own ruling. In 1793, the rule was changed so that only one Supreme Court justice had to be present at each circuit court, but the circuit duties were retained for nearly a century.

Initially, this was partly because there was little business for the Supreme Court to do—there were few cases in the court's first 10 years of existence. In fact, the justices did not decide their first important case until February 1793.

THE FIRST JUSTICES

George Washington remains the president who nominated the most Supreme Court justices. During his two terms, he chose 11 men to serve. The only president who comes close to Washington is Franklin D. Roosevelt, who during his 12 years in office nominated eight justices and appointed one associate justice to become chief justice.

As his first chief justice, Washington chose a wealthy New Yorker named John Jay. Jay hesitated before accepting the nomination, concerned that the salary was too low. Jay was certainly a fairly prominent political figure. He had been a delegate to the First Continental Congress in 1774 and had argued strongly against an attempt to achieve independence from Great Britain. Jay did support the Revolution after the Declaration of Independence was signed. He served as president of the Confederation Congress in 1778 and was part of the delegation that negotiated a peace treaty with Great Britain when the war ended.

Washington had offered Jay the opportunity to serve either as chief justice or as secretary of the State Depart-

John Jay was the first chief justice of the Supreme Court. He spent
much of his time, however, on diplomatic missions abroad, and
stepped down from the court in 1795 to become governor of New
York. Service on the Supreme Court did not hold the same prestige
then as it does today.

John Rutledge of South Carolina was one of the first six justices on the Supreme Court, but he did not attend a single session and resigned after a year. President George Washington later named him chief justice after John Jay stepped down. The Senate ultimately rejected Rutledge's nomination.

ment. Jay chose the first post but spent a great deal of time abroad on diplomatic missions and, later, on campaigning for state office during his term as chief justice. In 1795, he stepped down to serve as governor of New York.

Because Washington had chosen a New Yorker as chief justice, he decided to achieve some geographic balance with the five associate justices. His nominees were John Rutledge from South Carolina, James Wilson from Pennsylvania, William Cushing from Massachusetts, Robert H. Harrison from Maryland, and John Blair from Virginia. The nominees were confirmed by the Senate, but Harrison was forced to decline his appointment after five days because of poor health; he died two months later. In Harrison's place, Washington chose James Iredell of North Carolina.

These six men formed the first Supreme Court, yet their accomplishments as justices are dubious. Rutledge, a supporter of slavery, did not attend a single session of the Supreme Court and resigned in 1791 to become chief justice of South Carolina. Wilson speculated in land and bank stock and, when he could not pay his debts, became the first justice to be jailed while serving on the court.

These six men had all been supporters of the Constitution. The task they faced in that first Supreme Court was deciding how to apply the Constitution to the laws of the United States. It would be three years before they would decide their first case and begin the process of interpreting how the Constitution could and should govern the laws of the new nation.

3

CASES THAT
SHAPED THE
COURT

In the earliest years of the Supreme Court, the justices
met for two terms per year—one in February and one
in August. In 1791, when the nation's capital moved to
Philadelphia, the Supreme Court relocated as well, meeting in a room in City Hall. Epidemics of yellow fever frequently swept through the city, and the court was forced
on three occasions—in 1793, 1794, and 1797—to cancel
its August term because of yellow fever.

The first opinions of the Supreme Court were delivered
on August 11, 1792, in a case known as *Georgia v. Brails-
ford*. The case involved the debts owed by American

citizens to British subjects whose property had been seized during the Revolution. The state of Georgia had claimed the seized funds, and the justices agreed by a vote of 4-2 that Georgia could keep the funds until a lower court had completed its review.

This case is significant not only because it marked the first opinions delivered by the Supreme Court, but also because the justices made public the opinions of the majority as well as those who disagreed. At the time, each justice delivered an opinion of one to three paragraphs, one after the other. This practice would eventually change so that one justice would be chosen to deliver the opinion on behalf of the majority and one would offer the dissenting opinion.

In February 1793, the court's first major decision was announced, in a case known as *Chisholm v. Georgia*. Alexander Chisholm was a citizen of South Carolina who was suing for payment of goods that had been delivered to the state of Georgia. This case was an important one because it posed the question of whether a state could be sued in federal court by a citizen of another state. The court answered that it could, in a 4-1 vote. The states were furious at this ruling, and in early 1798, the Eleventh Amendment was added to the Constitution, declaring that states could not be sued without their consent in federal courts by citizens of another state.

TRANSITIONS

In 1795, John Jay resigned as chief justice to become governor of New York. Washington nominated as his replacement John Rutledge—the justice who had not attended a single term during the court's early years and who had stepped down to take a state judgeship in 1791. Because the Senate was in recess when Washington nominated him, Rutledge did serve as chief justice during the August 1795 term. When the Senate returned to session, however, Rutledge's nomination caused intense criticism.

It is interesting to note that Rutledge's poor attendance record did not spark the strongest criticism against his nomination. Instead, the senators' opposition focused on Rutledge's outspoken comments against the newly signed Jay Treaty between Great Britain and the United States (negotiated by Chief Justice John Jay) and on rumors of his mental illness. The Senate rejected Rutledge's nomination.

Washington then asked Justice William Cushing to become chief justice, but Cushing refused, saying that he was too old (he was 64 years old). Coincidentally, Cushing would remain on the Supreme Court longer than any of the original justices, serving for more than 20 years (14 years after telling Washington that his age prevented him from being chief justice).

Finally, Washington offered the chief justice position to Oliver Ellsworth, a senator from Connecticut. Ellsworth accepted the nomination and became chief justice in March 1796.

Shortly before Ellsworth's nomination, the court heard the case of *Hylton v. United States*, the first challenge of an act of Congress as unconstitutional. The case involved a fixed federal tax that Congress had placed on carriages, which was challenged on the basis that the Constitution required that all direct taxes be divided among the states by population. The justices ruled that the carriage tax was not a direct tax, stating that a direct tax only involved taxes on land and on individuals. This definition would be followed for the next century. The significance of *Hylton v. United States* is not the court's ruling on taxes, however, but instead its willingness to assume the responsibility of reviewing acts of Congress.

THE MARSHALL ERA BEGINS

In 1800, the capital was relocated to Washington, D.C., and the court once again moved. It was a difficult time for the Supreme Court. Chief Justice Ellsworth had been appointed a special envoy to France, and during the court's final session in Philadelphia—in August 1800—Ellsworth was in France, Cushing was absent because of illness, and Samuel Chase was spending most of his time in Maryland working for the re-election of President John Adams. Ellsworth became quite ill during his travels to France and resigned as chief justice in October 1800.

Once in Washington, the Supreme Court was assigned, almost as an afterthought, to cramped space in a House Committee room. In the fall of 1800, much of the new capital was still under construction. The plans for this new federal city were extensive, and great consideration had been given to the buildings that would become the White House and the Capitol, as well as to the shape and

John Marshall served as chief justice of the Supreme Court for 34 years, beginning in 1801. Marshall would reshape the federal judiciary and turn the Supreme Court into a true third branch of the U.S. government. The first major case of the Marshall era, *Marbury v. Madison*, established the court's right to declare a law unconstitutional.

scale of the boulevards that would radiate out from these public buildings. It demonstrates how insignificant the Supreme Court was at this time — the court was completely overlooked as plans were made for the capital city, and no building was set aside specifically for its use.

The rise of the Supreme Court to become truly the third branch of government is in large part the work of John Marshall, the man who became chief justice on February 4, 1801. Marshall would serve for 34 years and reshape the federal judiciary. His role was so significant that, of the 18 historical lawgivers whose figures are carved on panels in the Supreme Court chamber, Marshall is the only American, and the only one depicted for his work as a judge. Other figures include Napoleon, Charlemagne, and Justinian.

Most legal scholars agree that Marshall's role was tremendously significant, especially for what he did to ensure that the Supreme Court would be responsible for guaranteeing that the United States remained true to the principles stated in the Constitution. Marshall saw the Constitution as a fluid document—a document that needed to be able to reflect not only the United States as it was when the Constitution was first written but also as the nation would become.

Marshall's humble beginnings hardly predicted his future success. He had a limited education, and his law studies lasted only three months, while he was on leave from the army. It was Marshall's service under Washington, as a soldier during the Revolutionary War, that perhaps influenced him most strongly, causing him constantly to seek ways to ensure that the government remained strong and efficient.

With the very first case decided by the Supreme Court after he became chief justice, Marshall changed the procedure of having each justice read his opinion. Instead, a single "Opinion of the Court" was delivered, which announced the court's decision. In important cases, Marshall was the one who delivered the opinion. The idea was that the court would present a unified position on cases, speaking in a sense with one voice, and that unified opinions would be reached on decisions whenever possible.

Marshall took advantage of the fact that most justices came to Washington only for a few months of the year, while the court was in session. Their homes and families were elsewhere, and so they all stayed in the same rooming house and discussed their cases over dinner.

MARBURY V. MADISON

The first major case of the Marshall era, and certainly one of the most significant in Supreme Court history, came two years after Marshall became chief justice. With its decision in *Marbury v. Madison*, the Supreme Court asserted its power to rule on the constitutionality of an act of Congress.

The case involved one of the final acts of the administration of President John Adams. Adams, a Federalist, had lost his bid for re-election to Republican candidate Thomas

Jefferson. Adams was determined to make as many judicial appointments as he could in his final days in office. The Judiciary Act of 1801 created a number of new federal circuit court judges (to help relieve the Supreme Court of some of its circuit court duties) and also established courts in the District of Columbia, whose judges were to be appointed by the president. Adams quickly appointed more than 50 men to fill these new judgeships, all of them Federalists. One of these men was William Marbury, whom Adams appointed to serve as justice of the peace for the District of Columbia.

The Senate approved the appointments, and it became the responsibility of the secretary of state to certify and deliver the commissions. At the time, the secretary of state was John Marshall, who had recently been sworn in as chief justice. Apparently because of overscheduling, he forgot to have all of the commissions delivered. Shortly afterward, Thomas Jefferson assumed the office of president, and he ordered his secretary of state—James Madison—not to deliver them.

Marbury filed suit against Madison. Because the Judiciary Act of 1789 gave the Supreme Court jurisdiction in these cases against federal officials, Marbury was able to file his suit directly in the Supreme Court, asking the court to order Madison to deliver the commissions.

And so it was that two years later, Marshall as chief justice was forced to rule on a case that his mistake had helped create. The situation was a complicated one, made more complex because the suit forced the Supreme Court to decide what type of authority it held over the executive branch of government.

Thanks to Marshall's skillful leadership, the court was able to avoid a political fight with the Jefferson administration, yet cement its power in a more concrete way. The court's ruling found that Marbury was due his commission and that it should be delivered to him. The court, however, also ruled that it could not order the delivery because the Judiciary Act of 1789 (an act of Congress), which authorized the court to issue those kinds of orders against federal officials, was unconstitutional and void, an unacceptable expansion of what the Constitution declared was the jurisdiction of the Supreme Court.

With this decision, the Supreme Court retained—or perhaps confirmed—its power to review congressional acts and determine whether they were constitutional. It is interesting that the case, which seemed at first glance to be a test of whether the Supreme Court could review executive acts, proved to resolve whether the Supreme Court could review congressional acts.

A CHALLENGE TO THE COURT

This new flexing of judicial muscle concerned the legislative and executive branches, and an attempt was soon made to put a stop to it. Supreme Court Justice Samuel Chase, who had campaigned hard for the re-election of President Adams in 1800, had made an enemy of the man who won the election, President Thomas Jefferson, and Jefferson's fellow Republicans. Chase, an

ROE V. WADE

Throughout its history, the Supreme Court has ruled on highly controversial cases. One of the most controversial Supreme Court decisions involves the case of *Roe v. Wade*.

In its 1973 *Roe v. Wade* decision, the court ruled that most state laws outlawing or restricting abortion violated a woman's constitutional right to privacy. The ruling involved a Texas law that criminalized abortion, and the decision was based on the court's finding that this law violated the Fourteenth Amendment.

The decision has become one of the most divisive in American politics. Those who support *Roe v. Wade* often define themselves as "pro-choice" and believe that the court's decision helped ensure a woman's personal freedom and individual privacy. Those opposed to the ruling often define themselves as "pro-life" and believe that the court did not accurately interpret the meaning of the Constitution, nor did it consider the rights of the unborn child.

The "Roe" in the case refers to "Jane Roe," a pseudonym used for an anonymous woman who first filed the lawsuit. The "Wade" refers to Henry Wade, the district attorney for Dallas County in Texas.

outspoken and brash man, had in fact made several political enemies, in part for his support of the hated Sedition Act of 1798.

Article III of the Constitution specifies that Supreme Court justices shall hold their offices during "good behaviour." This vague term was used to justify an impeachment charge against Chase—that he had not demonstrated "good behaviour" in his often-thoughtless comments criticizing lawyers, defendants, and even President Jefferson.

The House voted to impeach Chase in March 1804, and the trial began in the Senate on January 3, 1805.

Controversy surrounding the U.S. Supreme Court goes back to its early years; one justice, Samuel Chase, even faced an impeachment trial because of the enemies he had made. Perhaps the most divisive Supreme Court action in modern days has been the 1973 *Roe v. Wade* ruling that legalized abortion in the United States. Here, demonstrators from both sides of the issue rally in front of the Supreme Court on January 20, 1998, two days before the twenty-fifth anniversary of the ruling.

Republicans held a clear majority in the Senate, and for a month the Senate heard evidence and arguments. Chase continued to serve on the court during his trial, and Chief Justice Marshall and the other justices attended the impeachment trial as a show of support for Chase.

In the end, the clearly political nature of the trial overwhelmed whatever evidence was presented. On March 1, 1805, Chase was acquitted; his opponents had failed to gather the two-thirds majority of votes necessary for conviction. There were rumors that the Republicans had planned impeachment charges against the other four Federalist justices, including Marshall, but the failure to convict Chase halted those plans. Chase would go down in history as the only Supreme Court justice ever to undergo an impeachment trial.

The trial was also significant because of what it meant for the balance of power in the American system of government. Impeachment could not be used to punish a Supreme Court that ruled an act of Congress or an executive decision unconstitutional.

THE COURT STRENGTHENS

With the tripling of U.S. territory during the first few decades of the nineteenth century (with the Louisiana Purchase and the addition of Florida), a new circuit was added—a circuit that included Kentucky, Tennessee and Ohio. To cover the circuit duties for this territory, a new seat was added to the Supreme Court in 1807, bringing the number of justices to seven.

In that same year, Aaron Burr, the vice president in Jefferson's first term, was forced to stand trial on charges of treason for his alleged efforts to encourage an independence movement in the Western states. The Jefferson administration brought Burr to trial, and tried to bring two of his accomplices to trial, as well. The Supreme Court intervened, saying that there was insufficient evidence to prosecute the two accomplices. Later, after the court's term had ended, Chief Justice Marshall presided over Burr's trial in Richmond, Virginia, as the circuit court judge. Burr was acquitted.

The first time that the Supreme Court struck down a state law as unconstitutional occurred in 1810, in the case of *Fletcher v. Peck*. The case involved the state of Georgia and a group of property owners who acquired land under a 1795 law that was later repealed, meaning that their titles to the land became void. The court found that the state's actions in repealing the law and voiding the land titles were unconstitutional. One of the victorious attorneys for the property owners was a Massachusetts lawyer named Joseph Story. One year later, Story would be appointed to the Supreme Court.

WAR AND PEACE
War with Great Britain occupied much of the court's business from 1812 to 1816, with cases involving seizures of ships, embargo acts, and foreign policy. The British burned the Capitol in August 1814, forcing the court to meet in several temporary locations (including a tavern)

This wood engraving depicts the burning of Washington, D.C., by the British in 1814. The U.S. Capitol was among the damaged buildings, so the Supreme Court met in various temporary locations for four terms.

for four terms. Finally, the court was able to move back into its courtroom in the Senate, where it would remain until the Civil War.

In February 1819, arguments began in the case of *McCulloch v. Maryland*. The case had its roots in the earliest days of the U.S. government, when George Washington's secretary of the treasury, Alexander Hamilton, argued for the need for a national bank. The answer in Hamilton's day had been yes; Washington established the first national bank for a 20-year term, and the bank's charter was renewed in 1816. An economic crisis, however, prompted several states to levy taxes against the national bank, including the state of Maryland. James McCulloch, the cashier of the Second Bank of the United States in Baltimore, refused to pay the tax, and was quickly sued by Maryland officials. When the case went to trial in Maryland, the state's judges ruled against McCulloch. McCulloch appealed to the Supreme Court.

The case of *McCulloch v. Maryland* posed two critical questions: Did the U.S. Congress have the power to charter a national bank? And could states then tax that bank's operations?

On March 6, 1819, the Supreme Court answered those questions. The court found that Congress did have the power to charter the national bank and to take any other actions that were "necessary and proper" and were not specifically prohibited by the Constitution. The states, though, did not have the power to tax that bank's operations, because by doing so they might make impossible Congress's original purpose in chartering the bank.

State powers, business laws, and taxes dominated much of the focus in the remaining years of the Marshall court. Federal jurisdiction over Indian tribes sparked conflict between the Supreme Court and President Andrew Jackson when Jackson defied court rulings by authorizing federal troops to force members of the Creek, Chickasaw, and Cherokee tribes from their lands. On July 6, 1835, Chief Justice Marshall died, leaving a Supreme Court far more powerful than it was when he first joined it.

4

CHANGE AND CONFLICT

To fill the post of chief justice after John Marshall's death, President Andrew Jackson nominated Roger B. Taney, an experienced Maryland lawyer. Taney was not confirmed until March 15, 1836. During the eight months between Marshall's death and Taney's confirmation, the Supreme Court met without a chief justice. The senior associate justice presided.

When he became chief justice, Taney was nearly 60 years old; he served for more than 28 years. Taney was the first chief justice to wear pants—before him, the chief justices had customarily worn breeches, short pants covering the hips and thighs and fitting snugly just below the knee.

Many of the cases the Supreme Court heard during these pre-Civil War years involved states' rights and contracts. Before President Jackson left office, Congress voted to expand the number of Supreme Court justices to nine. The two new justices were named by Jackson's successor, President Martin van Buren.

From the time of Marshall, a new tradition had arisen—to label the Supreme Court by the chief justice who presided, to distinguish one era of the court from another. The Taney Court was increasingly forced to deal with the emerging conflict between the states and the federal

This image shows a view of the Supreme Court chamber in the U.S. Capitol, restored to reflect how it looked in the period from 1850 to 1860, when it was last in use. Justices were seated at right, facing members of the bar at left center. The spectators sat on the lower left.

government. These issues gradually became connected to the explosive issue of slavery.

In 1856, the *Dred Scott* case was brought before the Supreme Court. Scott was a Missouri slave who had been taken by his master to live for an extended period of time in Illinois and other "free state" territories (territories where slavery was banned). Upon his master's death, Dred Scott was considered part of his master's estate and so was ordered to return to Missouri to serve his master's widow. Scott argued that the time he had spent in free territories meant he was now free. By the time the suit made its way to the federal court, Scott was suing for damages. He had become the property of his master's brother-in-law, John Sanford of New York, who had beaten him. Scott filed suit as a citizen of Missouri, claiming assault, but the U.S. Circuit Court for Missouri agreed with Sanford's argument that, as a slave, Scott was not a citizen of Missouri, and since Scott was Sanford's property, no assault could have taken place.

Many cases involving slavery had made their way to the Supreme Court, but the *Dred Scott* case was significant for the way it highlighted the question of whether a slave whose master brought him to a "free" state could be considered free. Also, it posed the question of whether even a free black man could legally be considered a "citizen."

The *Dred Scott* case was clearly an important one for the court, and the justices were not eager to rush their decision. Chief Justice Taney was also aging and in poor

Dred Scott was a slave from Missouri who had been taken by his master to live for extended periods of time in Illinois and other "free" territories. After his master's death, Scott argued that the time he had spent in free territories meant that he was free. The ruling in his case became one of the Supreme Court's most infamous decisions.

health, which did little to expedite procedures. Nearly a year would pass before the justices would even hold a formal conference to discuss the *Dred Scott* case.

Division among the justices mirrored the division among the states over the slavery issue. Taney determined that he should write the main opinion, but because of his illness, the final announcement of the court's decision was not made until March 6, 1857. Because of the strong sentiments of the justices, each of the nine wrote a separate opinion. It took two days to read these opinions in court.

The decision of the Supreme Court in the *Dred Scott* case remains a landmark, remembered both for its shameful conclusion and for how the polarizing issue of slavery was not resolved in the legal system. The Supreme Court declared that black people, even those who were free, could never become U.S. citizens. Further, its decision emphasized that the Missouri Compromise (which had divided western territories into "free states" and slave-holding states) was unconstitutional. What the decision essentially said was that blacks could not be citizens and that Congress did not have the power to stop the spread of slavery.

This judicial decision would not remain the law of the land. But it would take the Civil War to respond to the issues raised by the *Dred Scott* case.

WAR AND THE COURT

The *Dred Scott* decision and the division it fueled within the nation brought about a period of disregard for the

Supreme Court and its justices. In December 1860, the Supreme Court moved out of its former quarters, in the basement of the Senate, and upstairs to the room that had served as the former Senate chamber (The Senate had moved to a wing of the Capitol.) The court would remain in this location for 75 years, until finally moving to its own building.

In April 1861, the Civil War broke out. Justice John Campbell resigned because his home state, Alabama, had seceded from the United States. The other two justices from Southern states chose to retain their seats during the war. The court during this period issued decisions about the presidential war powers of President Abraham Lincoln and other issues involving the war.

In March 1863, Congress voted to add another seat to the Supreme Court, bringing the total number to 10. In October 1864, Chief Justice Taney died at the age of 87. The war was nearing its end, and Lincoln nominated Salmon P. Chase to serve as chief justice, believing that he would be able to support Lincoln's administration in legal issues involving the emancipation of slaves. He would serve until 1873.

Many of the issues that arose in the following years centered on Reconstruction, which involved the reestablishment of the seceded states into the Union after the Civil War. At times, the court chose to challenge Congress; in other cases, it refused. The size of the court was reduced to eight by the Senate in 1866 and then increased to nine after the election of President Ulysses S.

Grant in 1868. It was clear that these changes were politically motivated, designed to give certain presidents a
greater opportunity to influence the court by choosing
more nominees when seats became vacant or new seats
were created.

STATES' RIGHTS

As the Reconstruction era drew to a close, the Supreme
Court increasingly considered cases that reflected a new
balance between state and federal rights. With time, the
court gave greater weight to states' rights in many of these
cases. Morrison R. Waite, a lawyer who had no judicial
experience and had never argued a case before the Supreme Court, was chosen to become chief justice when
Chase died of a sudden stroke. Waite strongly supported
states' rights and felt that the court should take a narrow
view of federal privileges. Many of these acts involved
striking down laws enacted by Congress to ensure that
newly freed blacks were given the right to vote.

Melville Fuller became chief justice of the Supreme
Court as the court prepared to begin its second century.
The court, like the nation, would experience many tran-
sitions as it moved from the nineteenth to the twentieth
centuries. In 1891, Congress eliminated the law that
required Supreme Court justices to travel to the circuit
courts to hear cases. Instead, a new system of federal appeals courts was set up, whose decisions would often be
final; at times the Supreme Court could decide whether or
not to hear appeals from them.

One of the most important cases of this period was the case that sparked the phrase "separate but equal"—the case of *Plessy v. Ferguson*. The Supreme Court's decision in this case—which would become yet another landmark case in the civil rights struggle—confirmed the legality of a Louisiana law that required railroads in the state to provide separate cars for black and white passengers. According to the court, the law was designed to ensure that peace was preserved and, the court said, "If one race be inferior to the other socially, the Constitution of the United States cannot put them upon the same plane." Only one justice disagreed with the decision.

Oliver Wendell Holmes was nominated to the Supreme Court in late 1902 by President Theodore Roosevelt. He would serve for more than 29 years and is considered by many to be one of the greatest justices who ever served on the Supreme Court. The court during his time was largely conservative; he frequently disagreed with its opinions and his published dissents would later become the position of more modern courts. He served under four chief justices before finally resigning at the age of 90.

In 1910, Chief Justice Fuller died. His replacement was Edward White, who had served for almost 17 years as an associate justice. He was the first sitting justice to be named chief justice. He would serve as chief justice for 11 years.

The outbreak of World War I and the draft prompted new cases before the court, cases that challenged the rights of the federal government to create a military draft

Chief Justice William Howard Taft *(left)* and Associate Justice Oliver Wendell Holmes are shown attending a White House reception in 1922. Taft is the only former U.S. president to serve on the Supreme Court. Holmes is regarded as one of the court's greatest justices.

and to pass acts designed to protect the nation against espionage. One of these was the case of *Schenck v. United States* in 1919. Writing for the majority, Justice Holmes stated that when there was a "clear and present danger," the government might legitimately take actions that would limit the right to free speech.

Upon the death of Chief Justice White in 1921, President Warren Harding nominated a former president to be chief justice—William Howard Taft. Under Taft, work would begin on a building for the Supreme Court. Taft, a conservative man, inspired a more conservative court, which used its powers of judicial review to strike down numerous federal laws, including labor laws, regulations of spending in elections, and laws taxing child labor.

Chief Justice Taft resigned in 1930 because of illness and was replaced by Chief Justice Charles Hughes. The court remained primarily conservative, causing problems in the 1930s when confronted with New Deal legislation championed by President Franklin D. Roosevelt. Roosevelt tried to address this opposition during his second term, in response to his own frustration over the advanced age of the justices and, more important, their unwillingness to support his legislation. He sent to Congress a proposal for "judicial reform," asking Congress to authorize him to appoint an additional member of the Supreme Court for each justice older than 70 who did not resign. If the law had passed, it would have given Roosevelt the power to appoint six new justices immediately. Although Congress did not fully support the request, it did pass a law providing that Supreme Court justices could retire and still receive their salary. Roosevelt would have to wait, but after five years he would eventually name eight justices and elevate a ninth to chief justice.

In 1935, the Supreme Court finally moved into its own building. From 1937 to 1941, the court gradually began to support much of the New Deal legislation it had initially struck down. The court upheld the Fair Labor Standards Act of 1938, which prohibited child labor, set a maximum 40-hour workweek, and created a minimum wage for workers.

In 1941, Chief Justice Hughes retired, and Justice Harlan Fiske Stone, who had served for 16 years on the court, was elevated to chief justice. He would serve for five years before dying only hours after delivering an opinion from the bench. His replacement was Fred M. Vinson, President Truman's secretary of the treasury, who would serve until 1953.

CIVIL RIGHTS

In the 1950s, two issues dominated the court: the Cold War and civil rights. The Cold War rulings involved concern over the perceived threat of communism and laws passed to prevent its spread in the United States. The civil rights cases involved ongoing questions about the "separate but equal" ruling expressed in *Plessy v. Ferguson* more than five decades earlier.

Perhaps the most famous of these cases was *Brown v. Board of Education of Topeka,* which challenged the

William O. Douglas holds the honor of being the longest-serving Supreme Court justice. He served on the court for 36 years, 6 months, and 25 days.

Douglas was nominated by Franklin D. Roosevelt and was sworn in on April 17, 1939. He was a relatively young justice when he was appointed—only 40 years old—and he quickly developed a reputation among the justices as brilliant but eccentric.

Douglas was born in Minnesota and grew up in the state of Washington. He loved the outdoors but had polio as a child and was told that he might never walk again. Using courage and sheer determination, he began to hike in the mountains near his home to strengthen his weak legs, overcoming both his childhood illness and poverty to become an avid woodsman and a successful political figure.

When Roosevelt ran for his fourth term as president in 1944, he considered Douglas as a possible vice president. Douglas, though, remained on the Supreme Court, missing the opportunity to become president when Roosevelt died in 1945.

Instead, Douglas made his mark on the judicial branch. A firm supporter of individual rights, Douglas did not hesitate to make his opinions known, even when he was firmly in the minority. Over the three decades he served on the court, he wrote more than 1,200 opinions.

In 1969, Douglas faced an unsuccessful impeachment attempt from the House of Representatives. He was accused of endorsing "riot and revolution" in some of his published writing, of maintaining connections to organized crime, and of practicing law while serving on the bench.

Douglas suffered a stroke in 1974. Poor health ultimately made it impossible for him to continue to serve as a justice, and he retired on November 12, 1975. He died in 1980.

segregation of public elementary and secondary schools. The initial arguments were first made to the Supreme Court in December 1952; rearguments took place in December 1953. By then, the court had a new chief justice.

Chief Justice Earl Warren would become firmly connected to the civil rights movement for the many landmark cases that were brought before the Supreme Court during his tenure. He was appointed by President Dwight D. Eisenhower in 1953, when he was serving as the governor of California.

It was Warren who spoke for the majority of the court in 1954 when the court announced its unanimous decision in *Brown v. Board of Education,* a decision that meant the reversal of *Plessy v. Ferguson.* Warren's opinion included the critical words: "We conclude that in the field of public education the doctrine of 'separate but equal' has no place. Separate educational facilities are inherently unequal."

Other important decisions included the 1963 *Gideon v. Wainwright* case, in which the court ruled that states must provide legal assistance for all defendants charged with serious crimes when the defendants were unable to pay for legal representation. In 1966, the court ruled in *Miranda v. Arizona* that the police must first inform a suspect of his right to remain silent, of the fact that anything he says may be used against him, and of his right to have a lawyer, before that suspect can be interrogated. Any statements made by a suspect who had not been informed of his rights could not be used in a court case.

SCHOOL PRAYER

In 1962, the court ruled in *Engel v. Vitale* that a state could not dictate a prayer or other "religious statement" for use in public schools. The court followed this decision in 1963 by ruling that states could not require daily Bible reading in public schools.

The court's first African-American justice, Thurgood Marshall, was nominated by President Lyndon B. Johnson in 1967. As a lawyer, Marshall had argued the *Brown v. Board of Education* case before the Supreme Court for the NAACP Legal Defense Fund.

Justice Earl Warren announced his decision to retire in 1968. President Johnson nominated Justice Abe Fortas to be elevated to chief justice, but Fortas's nomination came under heavy criticism, and he ultimately asked Johnson to withdraw it. Investigations of ethical violations eventually forced Fortas to step down as justice under threat of impeachment.

With Warren's retirement, the newly elected president, Richard Nixon, nominated Warren E. Burger to become the fifteenth man to serve as chief justice. Nixon was able to nominate three additional justices, and the court quickly became more conservative than it had been under Warren. Nonetheless, the court supported busing and other methods to require school districts to achieve greater racial balance, supporting the decision in *Brown*. The court also overthrew a state law that discriminated against women.

The court's most dramatic ruling was in 1971, in a case based upon the publication in *The New York Times* and

One controversial case that the Supreme Court considered in the 1970s was *Regents of the University of California v. Bakke*, in which a white man charged that affirmative action resulted in "reverse discrimination." Here, demonstrators protest the 1978 Supreme Court decision during a march at the federal courthouse in New York City.

The Washington Post of a series of articles on the Vietnam War. The articles, based on a 7,000-page top-secret report known as the "Pentagon Papers," revealed how previous presidential administrations had misled the American public about the status of the war in Vietnam. The Nixon administration quickly moved to halt the publication of the articles, charging that they contained classified information. The court ultimately ruled that the newspapers could proceed with the publication of the articles.

CONTROVERSIES

In 1973, the court ruled on abortion in *Roe v. Wade*. The court overturned a Texas law banning abortion in a 7-2 vote. This decision would remain controversial many decades after the court's ruling.

When President Nixon's administration became embroiled in controversy during the Watergate scandal, Nixon's taped recordings of White House conversations were subpoenaed, to be used as evidence at the trials of former White House aides. Nixon refused to turn over the tapes, claiming executive privilege—the right of the president to refuse a court order on the grounds that it would harm national security or other national interests. In *United States v. Nixon,* however, the Supreme Court ruled unanimously that Nixon must comply with a court order to turn over the tapes. The information revealed on the tapes confirmed that Nixon had personally been involved in obstruction of justice; he resigned to avoid impeachment.

One other controversial case that came before the court in the 1970s was *Regents of the University of California v. Bakke*. This case involved claims of "reverse discrimination," in which a white man charged that affirmative action was giving preferential treatment to women, blacks, and other minority groups. The 1978 case resulted in a court ruling that so-called racial quotas were not legal but that race could be considered as a factor in college and university admissions.

The first woman justice was appointed in 1981. Sandra Day O'Connor was appointed by a conservative president, Ronald Reagan, but her positions on controversial issues were not reliably conservative. She became an important "swing vote," taking both conservative and more liberal stances on varying issues.

THE MODERN COURT

In 1986, Warren Burger retired and was succeeded as chief justice by William Rehnquist, who had served as an associate justice in the Burger Court. In the 1989 *Texas v. Johnson* case (a case involving flag burning), the Rehnquist Court ruled that the First Amendment's promise of freedom of speech protects even forms of speech that the court might find unpleasant or distasteful.

The Supreme Court also confronted free speech as it impacted the Internet in the 1997 case *Reno v. ACLU*. The court rejected a congressional attempt to regulate speech in cyberspace.

The Rehnquist Court was also forced to make a difficult decision about presidential immunity. In the 1997 case *Clinton v. Jones,* the court had to consider whether President Bill Clinton (or future presidents) should be protected from private lawsuits related to matters that had occurred before he became president. The court ruled that a sitting president had no immunity from such lawsuits. Chief Justice Rehnquist would later preside over impeachment hearings against Clinton, held in the Senate.

Supporters of presidential candidates Al Gore and George W. Bush argue outside the Supreme Court in December 2000, hours after the court heard oral arguments in the *Bush v. Gore* case. The court ruled that any further recount of votes in Florida should be halted, and Bush became the winner of the presidential election.

One of the Rehnquist Court's most significant political cases involved the 2000 presidential election. In *Bush v. Gore,* the Supreme Court ruled to halt any further recount of Florida precinct votes in the presidential election between George W. Bush and Albert Gore. The election had been extremely close, and the painstaking recount of votes in Florida had resulted in a delayed announcement of who had won the election. The Supreme Court's decision to halt the recount resulted, some critics charged, in the election being given to George W. Bush.

Chief Justice Rehnquist stepped down because of illness in September 2005. President George W. Bush nominated John G. Roberts, Jr., of Maryland to become the new chief justice. The Senate quickly approved Roberts, who took his seat on September 29, 2005.

5

How the
Supreme Court
Works

A Supreme Court term always begins on the first Monday in October. The Supreme Court continues to hear cases until late June or early July. Each term of the court is divided into "sittings" and "recesses." During the "sittings" period, the justices hear cases and deliver opinions. During the "recesses," the justices attend to the business before the court and write opinions on pending cases. During the term, the sittings and recesses alternate. Generally, each lasts about two weeks.

When the Supreme Court is sitting, the public sessions begin at 10:00 A.M. and last until 3:00 P.M., with a one-hour break for lunch. Public sessions are held on Mondays, Tuesdays, and Wednesdays. On Fridays before and during weeks when the court hears oral arguments, the justices meet in private to discuss the cases that are being argued before them and to discuss and vote on petitions for review—requests for the Supreme Court to hear a particular case.

When the court is in session, a marshal announces the entrances of the justices to the court at 10:00 A.M. Those in the court stand and remain standing until the justices are seated. The marshal announces the arrival of the justices and the opening of the court session with the traditional "Oyez! Oyez!" chant.

Before oral arguments begin, the justices first attend to any other court business. This might include the Monday morning release of the public report of court actions, called the Order List. This list includes details of cases that have been accepted and rejected and a list of new members who have been admitted to the Supreme Court Bar. Admission to the bar allows members to argue and file cases before the justices.

On the third Monday of each sitting, the justices assume their seats in the courtroom, but no arguments are heard. This is the time when the court's opinions are typically released to the public. Opinions are also released on Tuesday and Wednesday mornings.

Once all of the submitted cases have been heard and decided (typically in early summer), the Supreme Court sits only to make announcements of orders and opinions.

If all court business has been completed for the term, the court recesses at the end of June. This means that the spring is generally especially busy in the Supreme Court, with justices trying to complete their casework before the recess.

During the summer, the justices study petitions for review (they can receive as many as 150 a week) and make preparations for cases scheduled to be heard in the fall. The court can be brought back into session under extraordinary circumstances.

THE CHIEF JUSTICE

The chief justice of the Supreme Court, in addition to hearing cases and writing opinions, is charged with administering the court. These duties include assigning himself and his fellow justices to the circuit courts (as a circuit justice, a justice may have to issue or stay—meaning halt—an injunction or stay a scheduled execution) and approving regulations related to the court's building and grounds.

The chief justice administers the oath of office to each new president of the United States. In the event of an impeachment trial of a president, the chief justice presides over the trial, which is held in the Senate. This has happened twice in American history: in the first, Chief Justice Salmon P. Chase presided over the impeachment trial of President Andrew Johnson. In more recent history, Chief Justice William Rehnquist presided over the impeachment trial of President William Clinton. In neither case was the president convicted.

The chief justice presides over the Supreme Court when it is in session; he also presides at conferences of the justices when they meet to discuss cases. The chief justice, though, is often described as the "first among equals"—he is the chief administrative official of the court, but when the justices vote, the chief justice's vote is given no more weight than that of any of the other justices. Cases are decided based upon a majority vote.

John G. Roberts, Jr., was sworn in as chief justice of the Supreme Court on September 29, 2005, by Justice John Paul Stevens. Roberts is only the seventeenth chief justice in the more than 200-year history of the court.

If the chief justice is in the majority, he assigns the writing of the opinion to either himself or one of the other justices in the majority. If the chief justice does not vote with the majority, the justice with the most seniority in the majority assigns the writing of the opinion.

The chief justice also serves as chairman of the Judicial Conference of the United States. This is a kind of "board of trustees" for the federal judicial system. Members of the conference include the chief justice, the chief justices of the U.S. courts of appeals, a district court judge elected by his or her peers in each circuit, and the chief judges of the Court of Federal Claims and the Court of Customs and Patent Appeals. The chief justice also serves as chairman of the Federal Judicial Center—a research and training facility for the federal judiciary—and as overseer of the Administrative Office of the U.S. Courts.

Congressional regulations also specify that the chief justice has certain cultural responsibilities. He must serve as a member of the Board of Regents of the Smithsonian Institution, as a member of the Board of Trustees of the National Gallery of Art, and as a member of the Board of Trustees of the Hirshhorn Museum—the Smithsonian's museum of contemporary art.

ASSOCIATE JUSTICES

Nearly 100 men and women have served as associate justices of the Supreme Court. According to the Supreme Court Historical Society, the average term of service is 16 years. It is interesting to note that there is no constitutional or legal requirement that the justices be lawyers, although all of the men and women who have been appointed did have legal backgrounds.

Presidents have, in general, appointed justices who are from their own political party or who they believe will reflect their own political and legal philosophies. Geographical factors are also considered; presidents will try to appoint justices from different areas of the country to ensure that Americans from all regions are represented on the court.

For many years, the justices were all white men. Thurgood Marshall was the first African-American justice, nominated by President Lyndon B. Johnson in 1967. A woman was not appointed to the Supreme Court until 1981, when Sandra Day O'Connor was nominated by President Ronald Reagan.

A presidential nomination of a man or a woman to be a justice of the Supreme Court is no guarantee of their appointment. The appointments must be approved by the Senate, and throughout history, about one-fifth of all nominees have been rejected and others have faced intense questioning by the Senate. Presidents will, on occasion, nominate an individual and, if criticism of the choice is particularly strong, withdraw the nomination before the candidate actually faces the Senate.

According to the Constitution, the justices will hold their terms "during good behaviour" and can only be impeached for "treason, bribery, or other high crimes and misdemeanors." No Supreme Court justice has been removed by impeachment; in essence, the appointment is

THURGOOD MARSHALL

The first African-American justice of the Supreme Court was Thurgood Marshall. Marshall had made his mark on the Supreme Court well before his appointment as an associate justice. Marshall appeared before the court to argue the case of *Brown v. Board of Education*, the landmark case that shaped American civil rights policy for the next half-century, clarifying the idea that "separate but equal" facilities for blacks and whites would no longer be tolerated.

Born in 1908 in segregated Baltimore, Maryland, Marshall attended Lincoln University and Howard University Law School. He returned to Baltimore to practice law and was one of the few African-American attorneys in the city. Eventually, he was hired by the NAACP and began to work to challenge social injustice, segregation, and discrimination. Later, Marshall served as a judge on the Second Circuit Court of Appeals and as United States solicitor general.

In 1967, President Lyndon Johnson nominated Marshall to the Supreme Court. Marshall developed a reputation for being a plain-spoken justice with a strong sense of humor. His focus remained on defending constitutional rights and equality. He retired from the court in 1991 and died of heart failure in 1993.

In the eulogy for Marshall, Chief Justice William Rehnquist noted, "Inscribed above the front entrance to the Supreme Court building are the words 'Equal Justice Under Law.' Surely no one individual did more to make these words a reality than Thurgood Marshall."

for life or until the justice chooses to retire (often called "stepping down").

THE COURT'S STAFF

Besides the nine justices, many other people work at the Supreme Court. The staff numbers about 400 people and includes clerks and secretaries who work for the justices,

Thurgood Marshall is shown on October 3, 1967, his first day as a Supreme Court justice. Nominated by President Lyndon Johnson, Marshall was the court's first African-American justice. He served until 1991.

custodial, maintenance, and security staff, as well as many others who support the work of the court.

The court appoints a clerk to handle the mass of paperwork involved in conducting court business. The clerk (who has a staff of about 30) is in charge of recording, checking, and sorting the many cases that come into the court for presentation. In recent years, the number of cases coming into the court for consideration has risen to about 7,300 each year. (In the 1941–1942 session, the court considered 1,302 cases.) Of these, only about 80 will ultimately be heard in oral arguments. Each case might involve many different motions and numerous other briefs that must be recorded and sorted.

A significant number of petitions sent to the Supreme Court—some estimates suggest that it is two-thirds of all petitions—are from people unable to pay any legal fees or costs that their court case may involve. About a third of these are prison inmates. Some of these petitions might request the Supreme Court to overturn a death sentence.

The petitions involve many different kinds of cases. Some might ask the court to reconsider a criminal conviction. Others might involve racial discrimination, affirmative action, or family law issues.

The clerk is also in charge of receiving and processing the applications from lawyers who wish to be admitted to the Supreme Court Bar. The fee for admission is $100. Generally, about 5,000 lawyers apply for admission each year. About a third of the candidates wish to be admitted to the bar in person, during a formal ceremony, and the clerk must schedule those admissions. In this procedure, the chief justice greets the candidates before the bench, and then the clerk performs the swearing-in ceremony.

Being sworn in as a member of the Supreme Court Bar does not guarantee that an attorney will soon argue a case before the court. According to the Supreme Court Historical Society, some 225,000 lawyers have been admitted to the Supreme Court Bar since 1925, yet only a few of them ever appear before the Supreme Court again.

THE MARSHAL

It is the marshal of the Supreme Court who announces that the court is in session with the ceremonial "Oyez! Oyez!" cry. The marshal is also responsible for the actual management of the Supreme Court building and facilities—including maintenance, cleaning, parking, and telecommunications. The marshal handles the purchase of furniture and supplies as well as the contracting of any outside services.

The marshal is also in charge of special ceremonies. When new justices join the Supreme Court, the marshal coordinates these ceremonies. Similarly, the marshal is in charge of special events, welcoming important visitors and dignitaries to the court.

The court is protected by the Supreme Court Police, a special force of about 100 officers, who are in charge of providing security for the justices, their staffs, and all court personnel, as well as for the building and grounds. The marshal directs the court police.

The marshal also handles financial matters related to the court, including paying the court staff and paying the court's bills. The marshal must attend every Supreme Court session—it is the marshal who bangs a gavel to call the courtroom to order and who manages the timekeeping, the seating within the courtroom, and the recording of the proceedings. With the significance and wide scope of these duties, it is no surprise that the marshal's staff is the largest in the court. About half of all court employees work in the marshal's office.

KEEPING ORDER

Strict rules of behavior govern visitors to the Supreme Court. About 250 seats in the court are available for visitors. Visitors are not allowed to bring into the courtroom coats, hats, umbrellas, briefcases, books, cameras, radios, pagers, cell phones, or any other electronic equipment. All of these must be checked before visitors enter the Court Chamber.

In addition, visitors are not allowed to draw or make notes while the court is in session (this is only allowed in the press section). Visitors cannot whisper or verbally express agreement or disagreement with the subjects being discussed. Even draping an arm over the back of a chair is not permitted.

While the court is in session, the marshal's aides help attend to the needs of the justices. These aides are

Visitors to the Supreme Court wait in line early in the morning before the opening of the 1996–1997 session. Only 250 seats are available to the public. Inside the Court Chamber, visitors cannot whisper or voice an opinion about the matters being discussed.

generally pre-law or law-school students who sit behind the bench on small, straight-backed chairs. They might be seen passing notes from one justice to another or from a justice to someone in the court. They may be sent to get a glass of water or obtain a reference book from the court's library.

LAW CLERKS

The law clerks are perhaps the most critical element of each justice's support staff. The law clerks aid the justices in all aspects of their work, from sorting through the petitions for review to providing research, writing, and editing assistance.

U.S. Supreme Court Justice Clarence Thomas meets in his chambers with three of his law clerks. Law clerks assist the justices in every part of their work, from going through petitions to providing help with research, writing, and editing.

Clerks work side by side with the justices, although they do not participate in the court sessions or conferences in which the justices meet to discuss cases. Each justice selects his or her clerks, and the opportunity to serve as a clerk for a Supreme Court justice is considered a great honor for a law-school graduate. The work is demanding, and the hours are long. Generally clerks serve a justice for one year before going on to successful careers in law. Several Supreme Court justices previously served as clerks for other Supreme Court justices. The current chief justice, John G. Roberts, Jr., served as a clerk for his predecessor as chief justice, William Rehnquist.

The number of clerks assigned to each justice has risen in recent years, a reflection of the increased workload and increased number of petitions that must be reviewed. Today, each justice is entitled to hire four clerks, two secretaries, and a messenger. The chief justice is allowed to employ three secretaries.

THE COURT'S LIBRARY

The Library of the Supreme Court is an inspiring facility, with impressive rows of bookshelves, long wooden tables, and a high ceiling lined with lavish chandeliers. The court appoints a librarian, who manages a staff of 27 people.

The library collection contains more than 500,000 volumes, as well as computerized reference sources and microfilm. The library is available to the justices and their law clerks, members of the Supreme Court Bar, members of the House and Senate, and government lawyers. Journalists who regularly report on the court may make special arrangements to use the library.

6

How a Case Is Decided

Oral arguments of each case heard by the Supreme Court begin much as they have throughout the court's history. The marshal and the clerk still wear the traditional "cutaways"—single-breasted coats with a single button in the middle and a pair of coattails behind. Their desks are placed below the ends of the high bench where the justices are seated.

There are four tables in the chamber for the attorneys who will be making the oral arguments. In keeping with tradition, a pair of white goose-quill pens, crossed over each other, is set at each attorney's place.

The sounding of a buzzer alerts the justices to the time. They gather in the conference room. Again, in keeping with tradition, the justices must all shake one another's hands as a sign of harmony, no matter what the position each justice will take on a particular issue.

At 10:00 A.M., the marshal's gavel sounds and the arrival of the justices and the opening of the Supreme Court session are announced with the famous "Oyez!" (meaning "Hear ye!") cry. The justices move out from behind a red curtain and take their seats. The chief justice sits at the center; the associate justices are seated based on seniority, alternating between the right and the left of the chief justice.

Lawyers traditionally begin their arguments with the phrase, "Mr. Chief Justice, and may it please the Court...." The attorneys are given only 30 minutes to make their arguments, and they are frequently interrupted by the justices with questions or comments. If the questions from the justices have used up a considerable amount of an attorney's allotted time, the chief justice may offer the attorney an additional fixed number of minutes. A red light on the attorney's podium signals when an attorney's time has expired, and the chief justice will then interrupt with, "Thank you, counsel, the case is submitted."

This is how the oral arguments for a case presented before the Supreme Court are heard. But how does a case reach this stage? How do the justices decide to hear a particular case? And what happens once the attorneys have presented their arguments?

CASES FOR THE COURT

There are a small number of cases (usually between one and five each term) that automatically fall within the jurisdiction of the Supreme Court. The court is assigned to hear legal matters involving two states, or between a state and the federal government. These are known as "original jurisdiction" cases. The Constitution also specifies that the Supreme Court will hear cases involving "ambassadors, public ministers, and other consuls." In these cases, the Supreme Court is the first and only court—there is no other court to which the Supreme Court's ruling can be appealed.

The Supreme Court may also choose to hear cases from state courts. If a state court rules on a federal issue, and the person involved in the case has no higher state court to which to appeal, the Supreme Court may agree to hear the case.

The most common types of cases before the court involve requests for reviews of decisions made by federal appellate or district courts. If the court agrees to hear these cases, it will send to the previous court what is called a "writ of certiorari" (or "writ of cert" for short). This comes from the Latin phrase meaning "we wish to be informed." Essentially, when the court sends a writ of certiorari to a federal appellate or district court, it is asking to be informed of the details of a decision that court made or, in rare cases, the details of a case that court has not yet ruled on.

With more than 7,000 petitions coming to the court each year, a massive part of the court's work involves simply going through these many petitions to decide which cases to hear. Generally, the justices ask law clerks to analyze the many petitions and write memos summarizing the details of each one. Each justice must vote on each of the petitions.

Justices decide not to hear a case for many reasons. They may decide that the decision of the lower court was correct. They may feel that the case has no national significance. They may even determine that the Supreme Court does not have jurisdiction in a particular matter. If the Supreme Court decides not to hear a case, then the decision of the lower court is final.

A Supreme Court staff member delivers nine sets of documents to the justices. Each year, the court receives more than 7,000 petitions requesting it to hear cases.

IN CONFERENCE

A small percentage of the petitions—generally no more than 30 percent—make it past this initial stage. Next, the justices meet in "Conference," gathering in a special conference room to discuss the petitions and vote on whether they should be heard. The room is reserved only for justices; no one else may enter while the justices are meeting there. It is the job of the newest justice to serve as a "doorkeeper," opening the door when a staff member knocks and again waiting at the door if reference materials or other supplies are needed and receiving them when they are brought by the justices' staff.

Conferences generally begin at either 9:30 or 10:00 A.M. The justices must all shake one another's hands, and then they are seated at a long conference table based on seniority. The chief justice sits at the table's east end; the senior associate justice sits at the west end.

A copy of the agenda for that day is at each justice's place. If there is a case in which a justice may have a conflict of interest—perhaps he or she was involved in the case when it was before a lower court or has some personal involvement with the parties of the case—then he or she must excuse himself or herself from participating in that case.

Each case is handled in nearly the same way. The chief justice summarizes the details of the case, and then the senior associate justice offers his or her comments. Each justice comments in order of seniority. When each justice has offered his or her comments, the newest (or most

Justice Ruth Bader Ginsburg helps new justice Samuel A. Alito, Jr., with his robe just before Alito's formal investiture ceremony in February 2006. When the justices meet in "Conference," the newest justice serves as a "doorkeeper," opening the door when a staff member knocks or waiting at the door if reference materials or other supplies are needed.

junior) associate justice begins the process of voting on whether the court should accept the case for review. The other justices, in reverse order of seniority, then state their vote on whether the court should review the case.

At least four justices must vote to accept a case for review. If a case is accepted for review, then the attorneys are ordered to send a set of printed briefs (the legal documents presenting their position or argument in the case) to each justice. The justices receive these several weeks before the arguments are scheduled to be heard, so that they have plenty of time to review them.

ARGUMENTS

When the court decides to hear a case, the clerk is responsible for scheduling the case for oral arguments. It generally takes at least three months between the time the court agrees to review a case and the scheduled oral arguments.

Because the justices have studied the facts of the case from the legal briefs and from the initial petitions well in advance of the time the case is actually heard, many justices have formed opinions before any oral arguments are made. Only one attorney for each side may present the oral arguments, and they are limited to 30 minutes. Attorneys are not allowed to read their oral arguments, although they may consult an outline or notes.

Once oral arguments have been heard in a case, the justices once more gather in conference to discuss and vote on the case. The procedure is similar to that used when deciding to hear cases. The justices make their comments in order of seniority, and then reverse that order when voting. There must be a majority vote to decide a case, meaning that there must be five votes if all nine justices are participating in the conference.

THE OPINIONS OF THE COURT

Once a vote has been taken on a case, the writing of the court's opinion is assigned to one of the justices. The chief justice assigns the writing of the opinion if he is in the majority; if not, the senior associate justice in the majority assigns the writing of the opinion. In some cases, they choose to assign the writing of the opinion to themselves.

Both sides of the court's position are expressed in written opinions. Those who are in the minority choose among themselves who will write their dissenting opinion. A justice, whether or not he or she is in the majority, may choose to write an individual opinion if there is a special point in the case that he or she wishes to emphasize.

The opinion is, in essence, the court's legal explanation of its vote. It explains what the court saw as the legal issues in the case and the precedents, or previous legal rulings, on which the court's decision was based. The court's decisions are not meant to be based on the personal, moral, or political feelings of the individual justices but on their interpretations of existing laws and how they relate to a particular case. That is the purpose of opinions—to explain the legal reasoning that led to a decision.

Because these opinions are so significant and will be used to affect future legal decisions in other courts, the justices spend considerable time drafting and revising them. Once they are satisfied with the draft of their opinion, it is printed and circulated to the other justices. The justices then offer their comments, often requiring numerous rewrites of the draft opinions.

Once a justice is satisfied with another justice's opinion, the justice will indicate formal agreement by sending the author a note saying, "Please join me." This does not mean that the justice is requesting a meeting; instead, the phrase means something like "count me in." If a justice is not satisfied with an opinion, he or she may use the phrase "I shall await further writing in this case" to indicate that more work is needed before the justice will join the opinion.

No details about court decisions are ever released to the public before the formal announcement of the court's opinion. This is done in part because justices may change their votes when reviewing the drafts. This may even result in a shift in the vote on the case— the majority may become the minority and vice versa. When this happens, a new majority draft must be written and circulated.

When all the revisions have been made, a final version of the opinion is printed. The court's reporter of decisions adds a short note at the top of the decision, summarizing its major points, and includes a "lineup" that lists the vote of each justice. This copy—sometimes called a "bench opinion"—is distributed to lawyers and journalists once the decision has been announced in court.

In certain cases of major significance, the justices will try to reach a unanimous decision. Many believe that a unanimous decision carries more weight, making it clear that the Supreme Court firmly stands behind the opinion that has been expressed.

THE FINAL RESULT

The decisions of the Supreme Court have dramatically altered life in the United States. The rights to which Americans believe they are entitled are constantly being challenged, and rulings of the court have influenced their education, their voting, and their employment. The court has provided protection from discrimination and has defined the limits of police power. Court rulings have helped protect free speech and freedom of the press. The court has challenged Congress and presidents when it has felt that they have overstepped the roles assigned to them by the Constitution.

Despite the traditions that date back more than two centuries, despite the relatively small number of men and women who have served as justices, the Supreme Court does reflect an evolving America. New cases can cause a ruling to be reinterpreted. Certain issues continue to spark debate and discussion, long after a Supreme Court ruling—issues like abortion, prayer in schools, and the death penalty.

SANDRA DAY O'CONNOR

The first woman to serve on the Supreme Court grew up on a ranch in rural Arizona. Sandra Day O'Connor was born in 1930 and, until she was 7 years old, lived in a home without electricity or running water. As a young girl, she learned to rope and ride horses and to shoot a gun, but she soon discovered a love for the law. She graduated third in her class from Stanford University Law School, but many law firms refused to hire her because she was a woman. Finally, she was offered a job—as a legal secretary.

Eventually, she found work as deputy county attorney in San Mateo, California, a job in which she discovered a gift for public service. She served as a civilian lawyer for the U.S. Army and briefly managed her own law firm. She became assistant state attorney general for Arizona in 1965, and four years later was appointed to the state Senate.

Later, she served as a state judge and was appointed to the Arizona Court of Appeals. In 1981, President Ronald Reagan fulfilled a campaign promise to nominate a woman for the Supreme Court when he selected O'Connor. O'Connor developed a reputation as a "moderate conservative," often providing the swing vote on significant cases.

O'Connor served on the Supreme Court for more than 24 years. She stepped down in January 2006 to spend more time with her husband, who was suffering from Alzheimer's disease.

The Supreme Court provides an important third branch of government—a branch that can, and has, proven a check to the other two branches. But it also provides

Sandra Day O'Connor was the first woman justice on the U.S. Supreme Court, appointed by President Ronald Reagan in 1981. O'Connor, a moderate conservative who often provided the swing vote on significant cases, retired from the court in January 2006.

a last chance for an individual to seek "equal justice under law."

Former Justice Sandra Day O'Connor noted the key role that courts can play in providing citizens with an opportunity to protect their rights. In her book *The Majesty of the Law*, O'Connor wrote:

> It is the citizens themselves, through the courts, who enforce their rights. Enforcement is entrusted not to other government branches, agencies, or commissions that lack a personal stake in the aggrieved party's freedom but to the people. They take their claims to the courts, and the courts decide whether the actions of the executive or legislative branch have encroached upon some protected rights. The courts then have the power to halt the official conduct that violates those rights, and to order relief for past injury. Ready access to independent courts allows any citizen to press his or her claim. Even in the remote appellate part of the judicial system in which I work, any person, regardless of status or affiliation, may file a petition—handwritten, if the petitioner lacks the resources for a more formal filing—and that petition will receive careful and thorough consideration.

GLOSSARY

affirmative action   An active effort to improve the employment or educational opportunities of members of minority groups and women.

appellate court   A court that has the power to review the judgment of another court.

Circuit Court of Appeals   Any of the federal appellate courts, one in each of 11 judicial circuits, in between the U.S. district courts and the U.S. Supreme Court.

executive branch   The branch of government that is charged with such powers as diplomatic representation, the oversight of the execution of laws, and the appointment of officials.

executive privilege   The right of a president to withhold from the legislature or the judiciary certain important information relating to the activities of the executive.

injunction   A writ or order from a court prohibiting a person or a group from carrying out a given action or ordering a given action to be done.

judicial review   A constitutional doctrine that gives to a court system the power to annul legislative or executive acts that the judges declare to be unconstitutional.

judiciary   The part of the government whose work is the administration of justice.

legislative branch   The branch of government that is charged with such powers as making laws, levying and collecting taxes, and making financial appropriations.

monarchy   Undivided rule or absolute sovereignty by a single person.

New Deal   The legislative and administrative program of President Franklin D. Roosevelt designed to promote economic recovery and social reform in the 1930s.

opinion   The formal expression (as by a judge or a court) of the legal reasons and principles upon which a legal decision is based.

oral argument   Oral presentation of a party's position and the reasoning behind it before a court, especially an appellate court.

Reconstruction   The process after the Civil War of reorganizing the Southern states that had seceded and re-establishing them in the Union.

segregation   The policy or practice of separating or isolating a race, class, or ethnic group by enforced or voluntary residence in a restricted area, by barriers to social interaction, by separate facilities, or by other discriminatory means.

states' rights   All the rights and powers that the Constitution neither grants to the federal government nor denies to the state government.

unconstitutional   Not in accordance with or permitted by a constitution, specifically the U.S. Constitution.

writ of certiorari   A request of a superior court for the records of a lower court.

BIBLIOGRAPHY

Congressional Quarterly. *Guide to the U.S. Supreme Court.* Washington, D.C.: Congressional Quarterly, Inc., 1979.

Greenhouse, Linda. *Becoming Justice Blackmun: Harry Blackmun's Supreme Court Journey.* New York: Times Books, 2005.

O'Connor, Sandra Day. *The Majesty of the Law: Reflections of a Supreme Court Justice.* New York: Random House, 2003.

Rehnquist, William H. *The Supreme Court.* New York: Alfred A. Knopf, 2001.

Schwartz, Bernard. *A History of the Supreme Court.* New York: Oxford University Press, 1993.

Schwartz, Bernard. *Decision: How the Supreme Court Decides Cases.* New York: Oxford University Press, 1996.

Woodward, Bob and Scott Armstrong. *The Brethren: Inside the Supreme Court.* New York: Simon & Schuster, 1979.

Web Sites

Cornell Law School: Legal Information Institute
www.law.cornell.edu

Oyez: U.S. Supreme Court Media
www.oyez.org

The Supreme Court Historical Society
www.supremecourthistory.org

Supreme Court of the United States
www.supremecourtus.gov

FURTHER READING

Aldred, Lisa. *Thurgood Marshall: Supreme Court Justice*. Philadelphia: Chelsea House Publishers, 2005.

Hall, Kermit L., ed. *The Oxford Companion to the Supreme Court of the United States*, 2nd edition. New York: Oxford University Press, 2005.

Hartman, Gary, Roy M. Mersky and Cindy L. Tate, *Landmark Supreme Court Cases: The Most Influential Decisions of the Supreme Court of the United States*. New York: Facts on File, 2004.

Travis, Cathy. *Constitution Translated for Kids*. Austin, Texas: Synergy Books, 2006.

Web Sites

Basic Readings in U.S. Democracy
www.usinfo.state.gov/usa/infousa/facts/democrac/demo.htm

Ben's Guide to U.S. Government for Kids
http://bensguide.gpo.gov

Federal Judicial Center
www.fjc.gov

The Supreme Court Historical Society
www.supremecourthistory.org

Supreme Court of the United States
www.supremecourtus.gov

PICTURE CREDITS

INDEX

ABOUT THE AUTHOR

HEATHER LEHR WAGNER is a writer and editor. She is the author of more than 30 books exploring social and political issues and focusing on the lives of prominent men and women. She earned a B.A. in political science from Duke University and an M.A. in government from the College of William and Mary. She lives with her husband and family in Pennsylvania.